EveryDay MATTERS

a New York Diary

by Danny Gregory

Princeton Architectural Press
New York, 2003

Published by
Princeton Architectural Press
37 East Seventh Street
New York, New York 10003

For a free catalog of books, call 1.800.722.6657.
Visit our web site at www.papress.com.

Editing: Jennifer N. Thompson
Design: Danny Gregory

Special thanks to: Nettie Aljian, Nicola Bednarek, Janet Behning, Megan Carey,
Penny (Yuen Pik) Chu, Russell Fernandez, Jan Haux, Clare Jacobson, Mark Lamster,
Nancy Eklund Later, Linda Lee, Nancy Levinson, Katharine Myers, Jane Sheinman,
Scott Tennent, Joe Weston, and Deb Wood of Princeton Architectural Press
—Kevin C. Lippert, publisher

Library of congress Cataloging-in-Publication Data

Gregory, Danny, 1960–
  Everyday matters : a New York diary / Danny Gregory.-- 1st ed.
    p. cm.
  ISBN 1-56898-443-X (hardcover : alk. paper)
  1. Gregory, Danny 1960---Notebooks, sketchbooks, etc. 2. New York
(N.Y.)--In art. I. Title.
  NC975.5.G74A4 2003
  741.973--dc21

                                            2003013176

for pL & jack tea

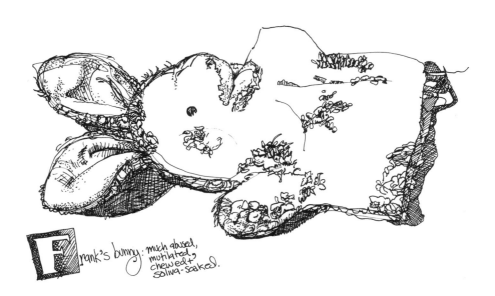

Frank's bunny: much abused, mutilated, chewed + saliva-soaked.

"Do not fear
mistakes.
There Are none."
— Miles Davis

a sweet toy.

ON THE STREET WITH MY BOY AND HE SAID, "DAD, YOU COULD DRAW MY HANDS IF YOU WANT TO." AND OF COURSE, I DID. WE SAT DOWN ON A BENCH ON 6TH AVE AND HE SAT VERY, VERY STILL WHILE I TRACED HIS HANDS. THEN HE HELD THEM UP AND WE LOOKED THROUGH HIS WINDOW.

I only started drawing fairly recently.

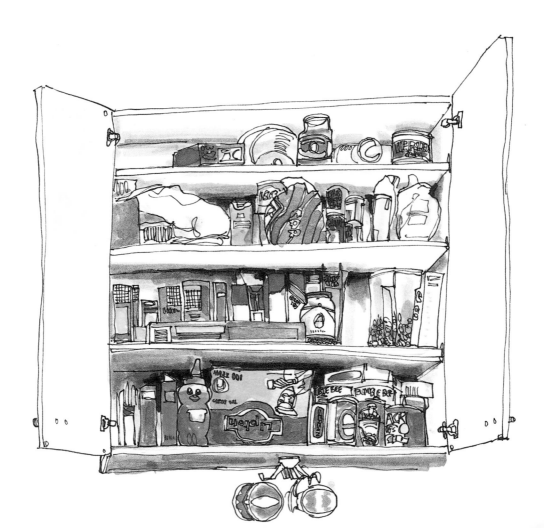

But I've found it has a power to change my life and the world around me so profoundly and I'd like to share it with you.

Before this story began, Patti and Jack and Frank and I had what we would have called a normal life in Greenwich Village in a nice apartment. Patti was a stylist, running around Manhattan collecting fashionable clothes and props for photo shoots. I was a busy ad guy, running around to meetings and shoots of my own. Jack was a little baby, just ten months old, busy figuring out how to walk. Frank was the only Zen member of our family, an eight-year-old mutt who knew how to relax. If you'd met us then, we would have told you we're happy but a little too busy to talk about it.

One hot and busy morning, Patti left Jack with a babysitter and walked to the subway station near our house; she was headed to a chic uptown bakery to get a cake for a photo shoot.

While waiting for the train, she fell off the platform and onto the tracks just as the #9 train pulled into the station. The engineer slammed on the brakes but too late. Three subway cars rolled over Patti's body, crushing her spinal cord and paralyzing her from the waist down.

Everybody we knew was stunned. Patti was vivacious, cute, stylish, and a new mom. This sort of thing just didn't happen to people like us.

IN the HOSPITAL, PATTI ASKED me **"WHY?"** WHY HAD THIS happened TO HER AND TO US? I SAID, "I DON'T CARE." If this WAS GOD'S IDEA OF A LESSON OR A PUNISHMENT FOR A FORMER LIFE'S TRANSGRESSIONS, WELL, I WASN'T INTERESTED. THERE COULDN'T BE AN explaNATION I COULD BE bothered to ACCEPT. I WAS DAZED AND MAD. WHAT I NEEDED to KNOW WAS "WHAT NEXT?" HOW DO WE REMAKE OUR LIVES AND BE HAPPY AGAIN? HOW DO WE GET OUTTA HERE?!!

18 WEST 18TH STREET

Patti and I met here and five years later (to the day) were wed here.

On every anniversary, we come back for a drink.. The year of the ACCIDENT® was the only one we missed.

WHITE RUSSIAN

ICE

MILK

VODKA

KAHLUA

While Patti was in the hospital, Jack and I logged lots of hours in our old cowBoy rocker. He would lean back against my chest, and we would listen to music or read a Book. When he fell asleep, I would rock and wonder what would Become of me.

I had no way to think about my Life anymore. I didn't know anyone who was married to a cripple. I didn't know anyone who was disabled at all. I thought of myself as this new thing, pushing a wheelchair around for the rest of my Life. All of our plans and dreams were Destroyed, and I was trapped under the avalanche.

Each day I rushed around, dealing with my job, with the Hospital, with Jack, taking control and figuring out logistics. But each night, I sat in the rocker, feeling sorry for myself in this Horrible new Life I had imagined for myself.

yogurt →

(There's cowboys on this fabric But I can't Begin to draw 'em)

After two months in rehab, Patti came home. Our apartment was a duplex, so I lugged her up and down the stairs to our bedroom. We began to develop new routines, reinventing even the most basic functions of life: getting dressed, cooking dinner, playing, making love.

The accident wasn't the only thing on my mind during those brownish days. I managed to start worrying about my job quite a bit. What was the point of my work? What if I got fired? Could we cope with being homeless?

My hypochondria began to flare up, and I suddenly wondered if something horrible would happen to my health next. And should we be living in the city? Would Jack become stunted? What was the point of life? Was love worth it if the #9 train could come along and take it all away? Was my existential angst just another burden for Patti?

Everything suddenly seemed up for questioning, and I was a mess.

MAN'S SEARCH FOR MEANING. FRANKL

How to Survive the Loss of a Love

HOLY BIBLE

A COURSE IN MIRACLES (OLIVIA... WILLIAM...

WHEN BAD THINGS HAPPEN TO GOOD PEOPLE...

C.S. LEWIS. THE PROBLEM OF PAIN

BORN ON THE 4TH OF JULY ~ KOVIC

SO, I LOOKED FOR ANSWERS IN ANY BOOK WITH A PROMISE ON ITS DUSTJACKET.

BBB

AT WORK, I made my colleagues nervous. If I tried to talk about the accident, about how I felt ... they fell silent. I could hardly blame them and was grateful that they obviously cared. It all seemed so vast, way beyond the small talk and gossip we usually shared! OUR FRIENDS WERE supportive. So was our FAMILY. But I had to tread a fine line. If I told them my life was a meaningless hell, they would surely have freaked out. If I acted like I was totally okay, I'd seem superhuman, out of the woods, or deep in denial.

mustifyingly
BLUE EYES

golden
HAIR

Patti's
Paw

better version of
looking up at me.

how jack
sees me.

Patti Enjoying a scoop.

WHILE I WAS LOOKING SO
FRANTICALLY FOR MEANING
PATTI WAS GETTING ON
WITH HER LIFE,

She was working, making new
friends, bonding with Jack,
healing. She was a new person to
me, with all of the things I'D loved
about her since we'd met comBined with NEW courage
and resolve. I was rather in awe of her and felt all
the more pathetic because, after all, the accident was
hers, and I was only a bystander, really.

A story a disabled friend told me:

A couple were going on vacation to Italy. For months, they'd been thinking about the rich food, the wine, the warm beaches of Capri, the bustle of Rome, the passion of the Sicilians. When they got off the plane, however, their itinerary had been changed. They were in Holland. Gray and flat. The people were bland and so was the food. Instead of beaches, there were dikes, for chrissakes.

The couple freaked out. This sucked. This wasn't the vacation they'd been looking forward to. They complained but nothing could be done. They were stuck in Holland. Tough luck.

But then something strange happened to the couple. They started to love Holland. The pace was slower and more mellow, the people radiated calm. They found a new world: Rembrandt and Alkmaar and hutspot and ancient coffee houses and the tulips of Keukenhof. In the end, they had a wonderful vacation. It wasn't what they'd been counting on. But it was great, nonetheless.

"Holland," my friend told me, "is where you and Patti have been dropped off. The world of disability. It's not what you'd planned on, it's not fast and furious like the life you led, but it is deep and rich and you will learn to live in it and to love it."

I've Always made things.

Little books, sculptures, meals, Doodles.
I've never thought o myself as an artist.
My father calls it "the curse of Gregorys," this
drive to always make things out of other things. My
grandfather spent years trying to make a
machine that would produce a little brass ship
when you turned its crank. He never succeeded
but his house was always full of partially formed
little brass boats. My father starts every single day
by painting a self-portrait and writes software no
one ever sees. My uncle is a potter and has loads
of kids. Eventually, a couple of years after the
accident, I found myself making things in earnest
again. I learned to bind Books. Then to throw
pots. And I wrote reams in my journals.

   Then one evening I decided to teach myself to
draw. I had always doodled on spare scraps of
paper, grotesque heads, spirals, grids, that sort of
thing. But now I committed to drawing the things
around me, sticking to studies of real things.

   My first efforts were Horrible. But one
quiet evening, I drew Patti while she sat on
the couch, out of her wheelchair.

LESSON 1

Something about that drawing was different from anything I'd done before. I took my time and then suddenly I zoned out. My mind went blank, my breathing slowed, and when I finally stopped to look at my page, I was amazed that I had managed to create anything so beautiful. At first it seemed a fluke, but then I drew the contents of our medicine cabinet (slowly, slowly), and again I saw something new. (You can see it, too, on the next page).

What was different was not the drawing but the seeing. I caressed what I drew with my eyes, lingering over every curve and bump, gliding around contours and into shadows. No matter what I looked at in this way, I saw beauty and felt love. It was very weird but it happened again and again. When I slowed way down and let my mind go, I had the same incredibly sensual experience. It didn't matter what I drew. And then I discovered that it didn't matter what the drawing was like. In fact, I could simply toss it away, like the skin of a banana.

What mattered was the slow, careful gaze.

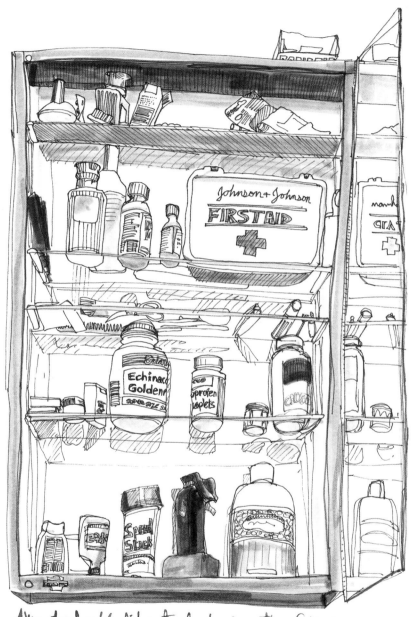

Why do people like to look in other folks' medicine chests? Here, look in mine.

The reason why most people draw badly is because they draw symbols instead of what they see. A nose is a sort of triangle. An eye is a circle with another one inside. An ear is a circle with a squiggle. The brain has an inventory of shorthand symbols for stuff, and that's what we draw.

It's very human. Assigning things to categories, using symbols and signs; these skills separate us from the beasts. Unfortunately, these symbols are a screen through which we come to see the world. We say, "that person is rich, that one's crass. He's a criminal type, she's a blonde, they're famous, she's in a wheelchair..."

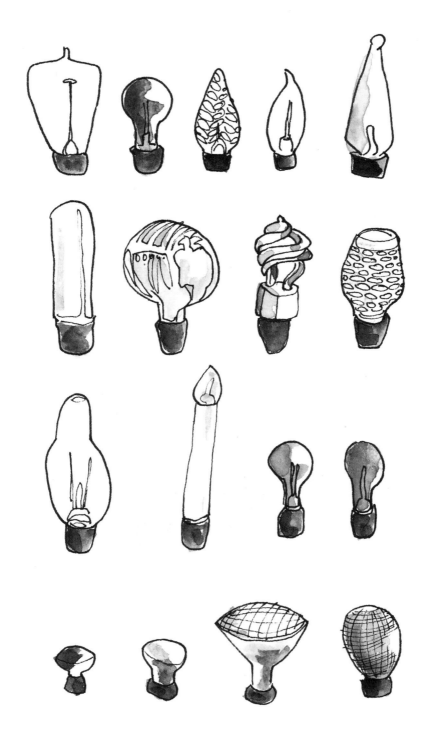

We lump people and things and experiences into categories and deal with them accordingly. It's efficient but it strips the world of texture and chance, like eating every meal at McDonald's or wearing the same uniform every day.

This kind of thinking shows itself when we try to draw. In fact, that's the reason most people will say "Oh, I can't draw." Kids never say that, until they reach the age of twelve or so, and their symbols are hard-baked.

What I began to see by drawing is that everything is actually special and unique and interesting and beautiful. Everything. Just by sitting and studying it, I quickly began to penetrate beyond the categorical imperative that made me feel so afraid.

I saw that if everything around me looks different than I think it does, maybe the gloomy life I had been defining for us was also just an illusion.

Because just as a tree is not a tree is not a tree, I had no real idea of what life with a disabled wife would be like.

I'd have to wait and see.

"TO SEE A WORLD IN A GRAIN OF SAND
AND A HEAVEN IN A WILD FLOWER,
HOLD INFINITY IN THE PALM OF YOUR HAND,
AND ETERNITY IN AN HOUR."
—BILLY BLAKE

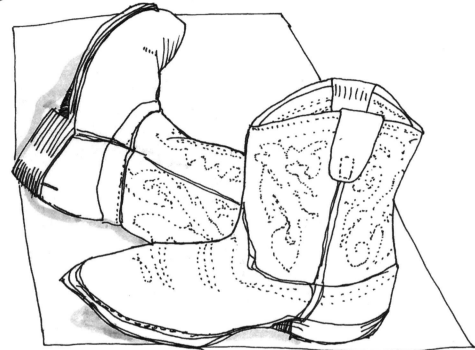

As Patti points out, it is difficult to tell the scale of these mini cowboy boots. Jack wears them, his leather vest, red cowboy hat, and Woody backpack whenever he decides to play cowboy. Then he takes the dog leash and chases FRANK around the apartment.

WE JUST GOT A NEW PILLOW

Jack asked me to draw his fire engine truck and fireman.

"i thank you god
for most this
amazing day; for
the leaping greenly
spirits of trees
and a blue true
dream of sky;
and for everything
which is natural
which is infinite
which is yes."
   —e.e. cummings

YELLOW-JACKET®

(x2)

He was lying on our
kitchen window sill,
a casualty of the
plunging mercury.

OR OUR COLLECTION.

Saturday.
Time to start
getting all
likkered up.
maybe start
a knife fight
or crash my
truck.

a chatelaine that used to belong to
Patti's grandmother in Cleveland.

my giant
STuFFeD
ROOSTeR watches
me eat DINNER
RESENTFULLY.

ReLax, man,
it's VEAL.

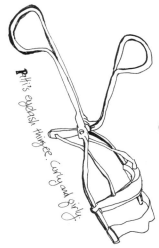

Riti's eyelash thingee. Curly and girly.

My drawings began as a way to count my blessings. To study, capture, catalog the things that, despite it all, make my life rich.

First my immediate surroundings: The sun, that falls on my notepad. Jack's new paintings on the fridge. The slow tumble of a dust bunny under the dining table.

I try to feel these blessings, to become part of them and their source, whatever that is. And that communion, not these drawings, is the reason why I draw.

o u r f a m i l y . .

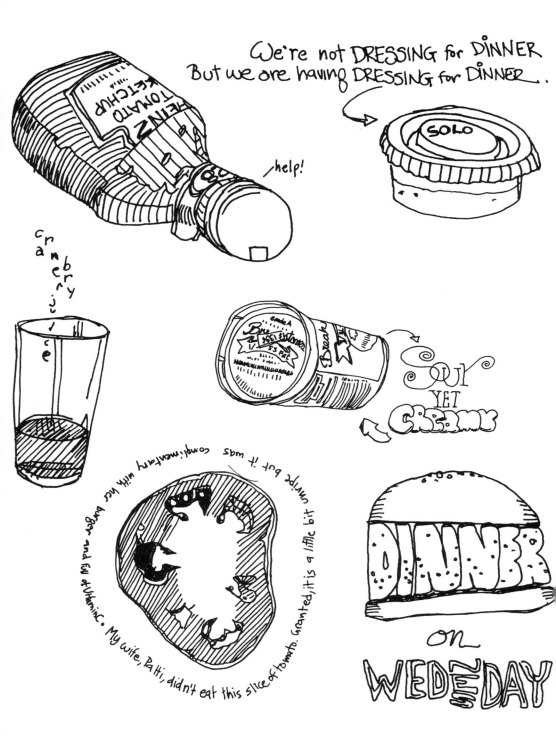

EVERY DAY MATTERS.

I think so. I do. But I really have to work to force myself to see its value sometimes. And drawing has really helped me to do that. Like, I often eat tuna sandwiches. But when I draw them, they stay with me.

I can ride the subway in a BLURR. or I can draw the wingtips across from me. When I look back at a drawing I did months ago, I am back in that moment, faster than a time machine, re-eating that tuna.

I had a sandwich like that once too. Burp. stayed with me for days.

The remains.

Everyone in our house (even Frank) loves to eat yogurt of all flavors and textures: Our favorites include: strawberry banana, blueberry, lemon, apple cinnamon, prune whip (?), peach, raspberry etc. I just saw that some sort of chocolate kind has appeared in our fridge. Wonder what that's about.

When I was a kid, this was a huge treat. My boy, raised on pasta from New York restaurants, won't eat this stuff. Weirdo.

One of my earliest memories is of Heinz Baked Beans. During a colorful part of my youth, I was kidnapped by my father and sequestered at my Nana's house. I remember playing with her tortoise with the hole drilled in the front of its shell where I could tie a ribbon, then coming into her cottage to eat beans on toast, washed down with very sweet tea. Very English.

I brought these from Paris.

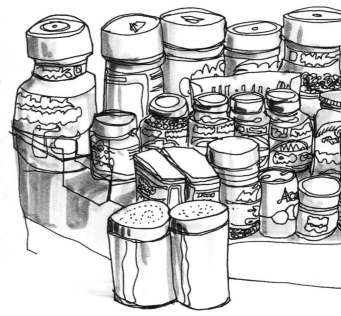

After four days of some really horrible drawings, I am sitting quietly in my kitchen, drawing all the cool things that sit before me. When the drawings get sour, life really feels out of the groove (or is it the other way around?). Anyhow, I feel better about the stuff I'm cooking up here than the way I've been seeing the world recently.

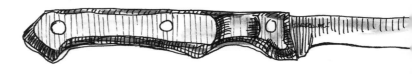

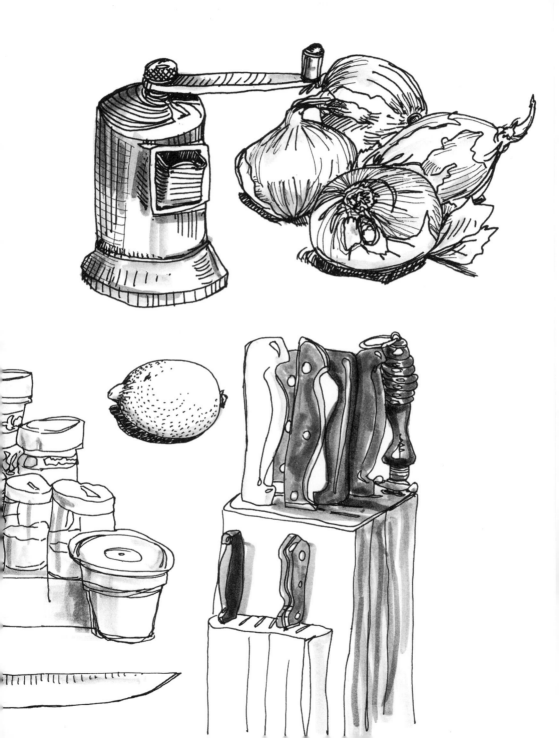

Ursus horribilus

I have collected taxidermy since I was twelve, and several rooms in our apartment are crowded with heads and little bodies. I have never killed any critter myself, and most of the specimens I own died before I was born but I'm not entirely sure about the ethics of the whole thing. The beasts in the foyer tend to freak out delivery guys, giving them something to ponder while I look around for change.

brown skunk
that lives in our vestibule.

Creepy Weirdo, the muskrat with the serpentine tail
(Ondatra Zibethicus)

quail.

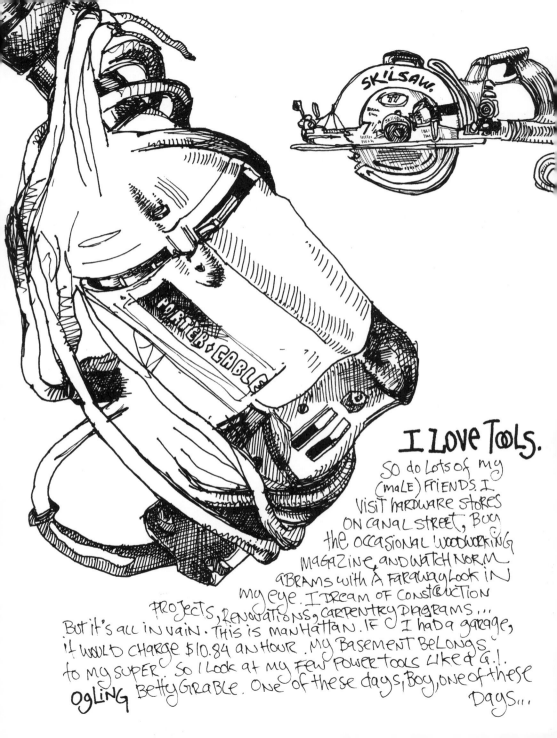

I LOVE TOOLS.
So do Lots of my (maLE) FriENDS. I visit hardware stores on Canal Street, Buy the occasional woodworking magazine, and watch Norm Abrams with a faraway look in my eye. I dream of construction projects, renovations, carpentry diagrams... But it's all in vain. This is Manhattan. IF I had a garage, it would charge $10.84 an hour. My Basement Belongs to my super. So I Look at my few power tools Like a G.I. ogling Betty Grable. One of these days, Boy, one of these Days...

Patti Bought this lantern for our patio this summer. WE ONLY used it a couple of times. It gives surprisingly bright and white light but makes me very NERVOUS. I imagine it falling to the floor and, as lamp oil (lemon scented) glugs over the glass, strewn redwood floor boards, OUR dream apartment will be consumed by relentless, lemon scented flames. + the fact that people have used this sort of lantern for centuries does not assuage my anxiety. I keep thinking of the great Chicago FIRE.

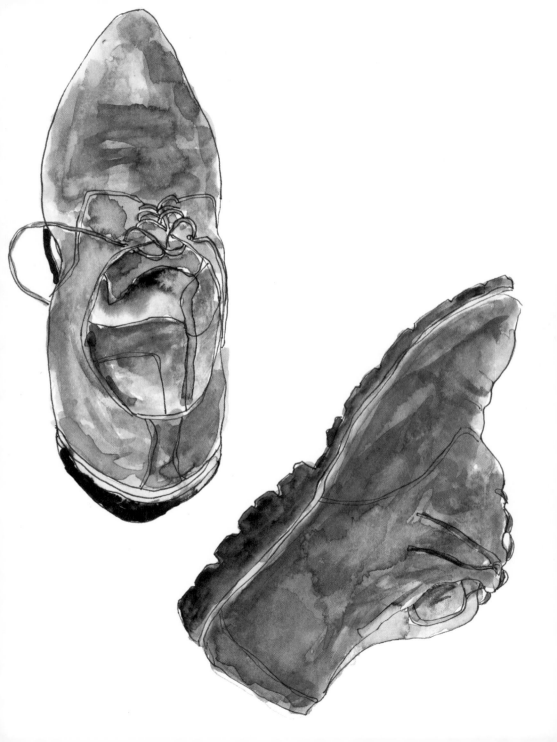

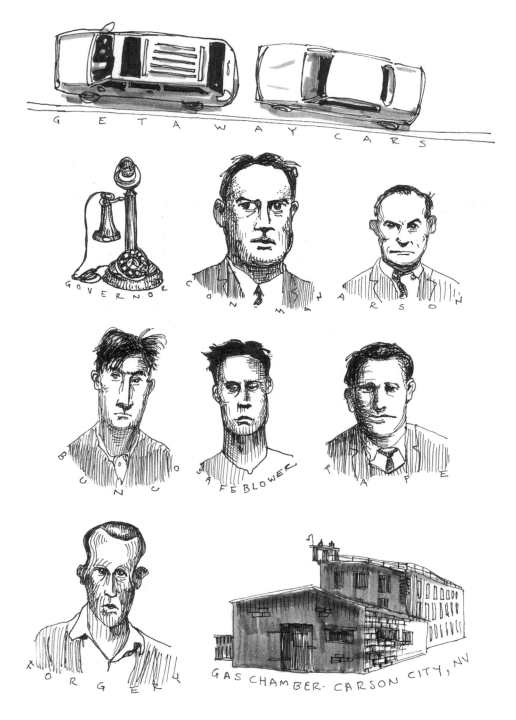

GETAWAY CARS

GOVERNOR   CON-MAN   ARSON

BUNCO   SAFEBLOWER   TAPE

FORGER   GAS CHAMBER· CARSON CITY, NV

I think I now know what has been troublin, me about doing drawings from published photos, and it is abundantly clear in the drawings on this page. Looking at a photo is looking at how someone else saw something. So my drawings become imitations rather than revelations, and consequently I feel like I'm cheating or cheated of a true drawing experience. This is particularly true of stylized photos. They tend to make me draw in a stylized and contrived way. I merged four shots of trumpet players into some sort of arty pastiche you might see hanging in a Holiday Inn cocktail lounge. It's not honest drawing.

Interestingly, if I draw from my own photos, my own vision, the feeling is less extreme.

TIME to GET OUT.

I've drawn every damned thing in our apartment, from the shoe trees to the ice trays. I feel like it's time to feel a little less safe and see how I deal.

At first I was really anxious about drawing in public. I felt like a poseur, pretending to be some sort of 'artist'.

East from Sixth Avenue

West from Sixth Avenue

Jack said this is his office.

And that anxiety made it hard to let go enough to actually draw halfway decently.

So I've begun drawing surreptitiously, sitting on remote benches in the park or in coffee-shop window booths. And, frankly, no one cares. There aren't huge crowds gathering around me to see how lame my drawings are and asking to see my artistic license. This is New York and to each his own.

New York is my home. When I was twelve, we arrived in the harbor after a week at sea on the S.S. Rafaello, statue of Liberty greeting us in the dawn mist, huddled masses, the whole deal. And, except

Broadway & Fifth Avenue at 23rd   Renovation on Fifth Ave.

for college (just 60 miles away), I haven't lived anywhere else since.

I thought I knew it really well but it turned out I've never actually seen New York at all.

When you look at something, you are filing it into a category.
"I'm in the Park." "Here's SoHo." "Light's green." It's easy, it's
fast, it's the way to cope with a whirlwind like NYC. But when
you just let yourself SEE, it's like opening a window on the first
nice day of Spring. Things flow in, unexpected, sharp, differentiated.

Instead of whipping past, you study things you didn't really
know existed. The shape of a paint flake, how people stand on a
corner, a bush's shadow on a tree trunk. You allow yourself to
lose all preconceptions, to shed judgment, and embrace possibility.
Time's tyranny is suspended. Everything is beautiful in its
complexity and singularity. You don't need to draw to see.

But I do.

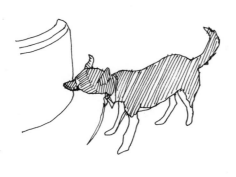

Every morning in th

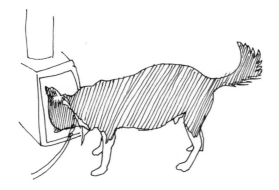

PaRR with Frankie.

Sometimes reading the newspaper can be like some sort of life sentence. Each morning, I carry exactly the right change I can efficiently buy the day's issue on the way to the subway. Then I try to race through all five sections and a hundred or so pages before the train rolls into my station. If I fail, I must carry the remains into my office where they loll around until I throw them in the trash when I leave for the day.

The weekends are even worse. The Sunday paper takes two days just to arrive, a fist thick slab of required reading. Patti often keeps unread portions around for weeks until she can bring herself to recycle them. Despite all this effort, I usually feel butt ignorant and uninformed.

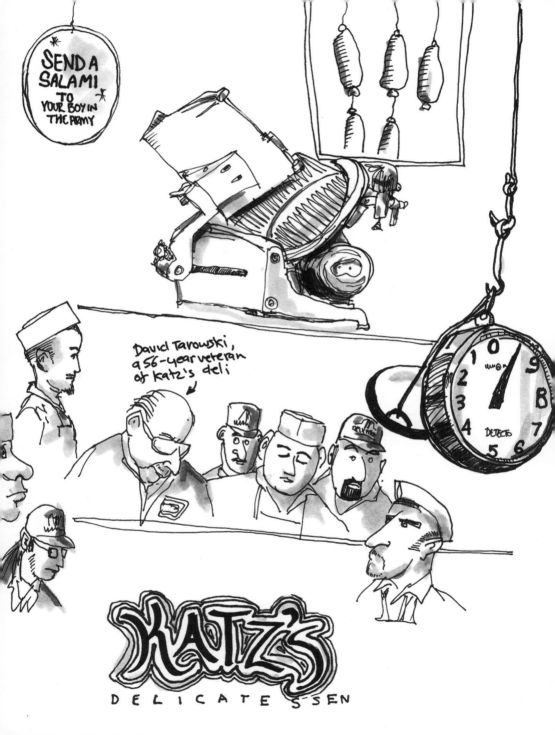

Most newsstands, like this one on MacDougal Street, seem to do a far more brisk business in lottery tickets than magazines. They are always run by Indians or Pakistanis. I wondered if they ever bought lottery tickets themselves so I showed this particular man my drawing, and he told me that he's from Bangladesh and has often won $60 to $100 in the lottery. I'm not sure how I feel about this.

Booths
and the people who work in them

The man who mans this cart had abandoned it when I drew it on Thursday morning. People stopped by but no one filched a cruller. Later I saw him walking down West 3rd with a water cooler on his shoulder. A trusting soul.

You can't use tokens anymore, just Metrocards. I have finally learned to trust those flimsy plastic wafers. More sanitary, less Noo Yawk.

This parking-lot booth is just off Eighth Ave. It seems like a really great place to work. I am applying for a position next week.

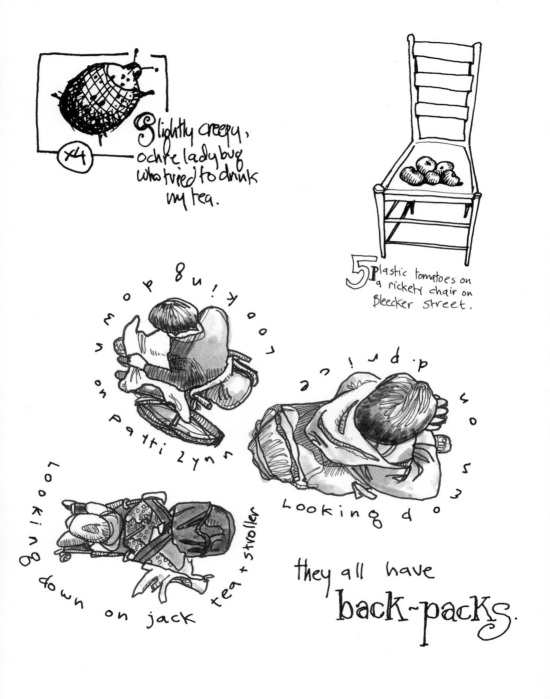

Slightly creepy, ochre ladybug who tried to drink my tea.

x4

5 Plastic tomatoes on a rickety chair on Bleecker street.

looking down on Patti Lynn

looking up once so 3 os

Looking do o

looking down on jack tea + stroller

they all have back-packs.

JACK

reading "Mama Zooms," the story of a little boy who rides around on his mother's lap in her wheelchair. He listened to the tape of the text being read while he looked at the pictures, turning the pages in perfect synchronization. When the tape was over, he asked to listen to it again.

stunted

People lining up for coffee and donuts at a ubiquitous "Good Morning" cart

These Exit turnstiles are sometimes creepy, sometimes scary meat slicers.

23 Street Station
uptown & Queens only
Ⓝ Ⓡ

I still find myself calling this line the "Double R". Makes me feel like an old-time New Yawker. I like that.

Riding the Rails

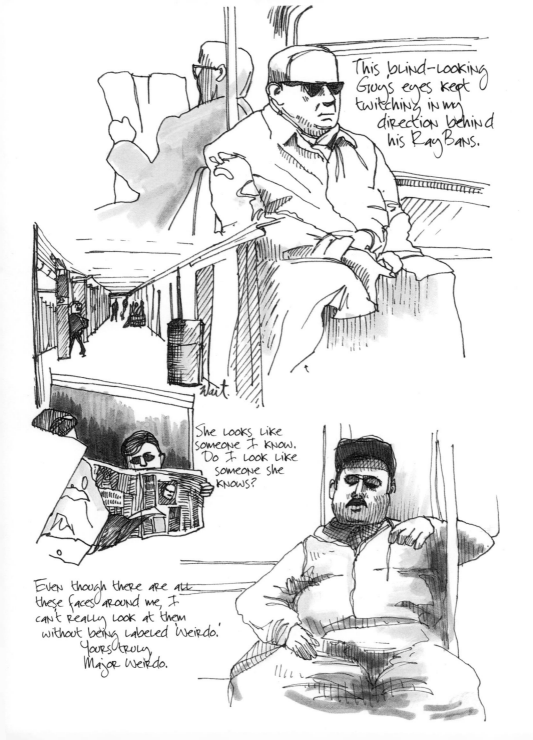

This blind-looking guy's eyes kept twitching in my direction behind his RayBans.

wait.

She looks like someone I know. Do I look like someone she knows?

Even though there are all these faces around me, I can't really look at them without being labeled 'weirdo.'
Yours truly
Major Weirdo.

I love how nostalgic and emotional the porno theatres are getting as they close down to make way for the squeaky clean new Times Square.

PEEPLAND
NON REFUNDABLE TOKEN

Thi
wa
sca

my office—

BAR
PRODUCTIONED

McHALE'S STEAKS RESTAUR

The cheeseburgers in this joint have done irreperable damage to my health.

BAR

← Now, I'll never get to go to the movies here. Darn it!

OOD TWIN THEATRES

EIGHBORHOOD

HK's Kitchen

I pass this bar on the way from the subway each day, year after year. Never been in. yet.

e ITWORK at.

CENTURY
PAWN BROKERS

LOANS

Jack picked each
of these leaves
for me to draw
in the park.
He decided my
drawings look
better than the
dry, brown, old
leaves.

Saturday in the playground

New York has zillions of trees.

I've never been as aware of them as I've become since I started drawing. They line our street and fill the plaza across the road! We look over a lake of them, Washington Square Park, and for the first time, we actually own two trees. One, our crab apple tree has gone from a distorted, twisted stick into a lush mini-tree laden with cherry-sized fruit. The other is a Hollywood pine, and it's gone from a black clump of Brillo into a little Christmas tree.

Last weekend I came upon a gigantic willow tree on 9th Street and Avenue C. It was at least five stories tall and almost half a block in width and depth. I've always loved willows — at Camp Trywoodie, we used to strip the branches of leaves and crack them: long, verdant whips.

Now the elm trees are giving up their leaves all over the neighborhood, and the park matches Patti's hair, a shimmering palette of copper, mustard, chestnut, and auburn. Soon, too soon, the trees will be nude again.

A good way to learn to draw trees is to study their bare limbs to really see how they are put together. I could use a lesson or two in tree drawing so I guess I'll buy some fingerless gloves and spend the winter in the park. I wonder if my pens will still flow smoothly when the mercury drops.

SOMETIMES I PITY TREES.

We stopped in for a drink and a salad (we're on diets). The bartender is

talking about how much he drank last night. Last time we were here, I swear, he was saying the same thing.

LATER: One of the waiters asked to see my drawing, then showed it to the bartender! I was mortified, he looked even greener. I should leave my journal at home, I guess.

wow! really good drawing, man.

3

I DECIDED TO TRY OUT a LIFE DRAWING CLASS. I SPENT a COUPLE OF HOURS OR SO DRAWING this WOMAN. AFTERWARDS, I thought, "It's quite a good DRAWING BUT WHO IS THIS WOMAN? WHY is SHE HERE IN my JOURNAL? BESIDES SITTING STILL FOR an UNNATURALLY LONG TIME FOR ME, WE HAVE NO RELATIONSHIP. WHAT'S THE POINT?" MAYBE I SHOULD DRAW NUDES.

OUR CHECK wasn't that much but the TIP was

WELCOME TO THE
HELL IS OTHER PEOPLE®
PAGE.
NOW, GO AWAY.

We waited for free tickets to the Shakespeare festival in Central Park. I would gladly have paid Broadway prices to shut the 2 people behind us up. I have never heard such obnoxious, self-involved nonsense in my life. God, I sound awful. Sorry.

Sometimes...

...i feel like this.

CONFESSIONS OF A BOOK FIEND

TRIED to CONTROL my PROBLEM BY switching to LIBRARY BOOKS at MY LOCAL, JEFFERSON MARKET. BUT BECAUSE I MUST READ A HALF DOZEN BOOKS at the same TIME, I O.D.'ed ON LATE FINES.

DER STRAND

Sixteen miles of used books and not a single civil employee. Still you can find some awful good books, at decentish prices. It's a lot of work, though. Uncomfortable, dirty, and badly organized. So I only come here once per weekend. Alright...twice.

MOTHER LODE

This is Barnes and Noble on the north side of Union Square and the biggest bookstore in all of New York. I am unapologetic in my wild enthusiasm for megabookshops. I come here far more than is healthy and can browse for three or four hours + not buy nothing.

And now my poor boy is hooked too.

BRUNCH
with the
HELL'S ANGELS

Sitting on my nerdy little folding stool and drawing the headquarters of the N.Y. chapter of the Hell's Angels, I felt a little nervous. I figured it was only noon on Sunday morning so they were all probably still sleeping off a night's worth of raging + pillaging. Still, they could burst out of HQ at any moment + snap my marker in half + kick my stool out from under me. So, laughing in the face of near dismemberment, I drew on.

I'm in my office, waiting for a CONFERENCE CALL

nat was supposed to happen hours ago. I wanna go home.

I HAVE A NEW TIC IN THE MIDDLE OF MY FOREHEAD.
I HAVE COME TO ACCEPT THAT I (PROBABLY) DON'T HAVE
PARKINSON'S DISEASE BUT THAT PATTI'S WHEELCHAIR
HANDLES HAVE PUT UNHEALTHY PRESSURE ON MY
THUMBS AND PALMS AND CAUSED THE MUSCLES TO STRUGGLE
FOR CONTROL AND THUS THE VAGUE TREMOR I SOMETIMES
HAVE, PARTICULARLY IN MY RIGHT CLAW. I DON'T LET
MYSELF GET ANGRY ABOUT IT, IT FEELS SO POINTLESS.
THE FACT IS OUR LIVES WOULD BE DIFFERENT IF
PATTI WASN'T DISABLED. WE COULD BE MORE SPONTANEOUS,
COULD DO A LOT MORE TOGETHER, COULD HAVE A MORE
EQUITABLE RELATIONSHIP. BUT WITH THOSE LOSSES
HAVE COME EXPERIENCES THAT HAVE BROUGHT US EVEN
MORE CLOSELY TOGETHER — SOLIDARITY, A SLOWNESS,
EXPERIENCES WITH OTHERS, A GENTLENESS AND SELF=
SUFFICIENCY IN JACK, A FEELING OF ENTITLEMENT,
A LINK BETWEEN US FOR
HAVING SURVIVED. I
have always tried
to stop myself
from getting
into self-pity,
FEARING I might
NEVER EMERGE,
though I HAVE
ENJOYED the
FRESH RAIN feeling
that comes after
CRYING. CAN I GO
THERE AGAIN? I
CAN DO ANYTHING.

I AM HAPPY FOR WHAT WE HAVE LEFT BEHIND but RESENTFUL DEEP DOWN FOR THE SACRIFICES WE BOTH HAVE to MAKE. DID I USED to ENJOY LIFE MORE? DID I USED to FEEL LESS BURDENED BEFORE? I DON'T REMEMBER. I KNOW that DRAWING and MAKING things IS A LOT LESS SELF-CONSCIOUS THAN IT USED TO BE, THAT I'VE COME TO ENJOY STOPPING to SMELL THE ROSES A LOT MORE. OR AM I BULLSHITING myself?

It's true that
i sometimes
can't separate
WHAT I
actually
FEEL
FROM
WHAT
I
KNOW
I'M SUPPOSED to FEEL.

I ALSO WISH I WASN'T FLOUNDERING IN SEARCH OF X AS MUCH AS I AM, AND COULD BE MORE CONFIDENT in my FEELINGS, AS A MAN OF MY AGE AND WRINKLEDNESS OUGHTA BE.

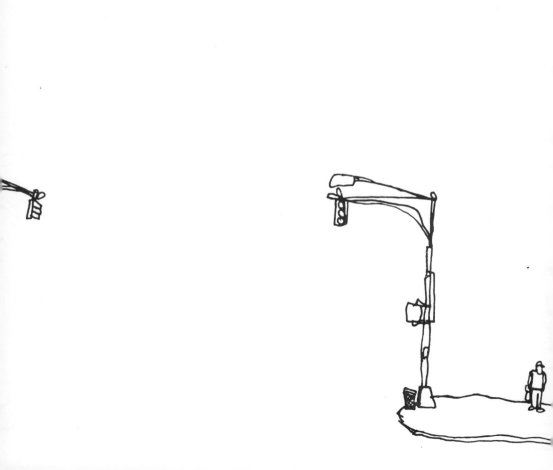

YOU SIT and STARE at something
Long enough, and it starts to come to life.
I've become preoccupied with the stories
behind the things I am drawing.

I've hunted Down and drawn places
alive with ghosts, Looking for the stories
under their skins. The more gruesome the
history, the more intense the drawing
experience.

It isn't really meditating so
much as rubbernecking.
Still it makes ordinary brick
and brownstone a lot more
interesting to draw.

Did something move behind
that window? Is that blood
on the wall? Heh, heh.

a ghost

scared MARK TWAIN'S WIFE out of this house (14 W. 10 street). A few decades later, a tenant wrote a book describing the grisly Victorian murder that occurred here. Soon after writing the book, the author killed herself. Various other weird things in its history sent a local TV newscrew over to interview tenants in the 1980's. A lawyer who lived here at the time told the TV guys nothing weird happened here. That lawyer: JOEL STEINBERG! Soon after, he + Hedda made the front pages for what they did

HERE →
creeparoorey.

Down on Julie Georg's art farm Patti DRIVes aROUND all day ON a LAWN mOWeR tRactoR; NOt to cut the 42 acres oF vegetATioN but to visiT the RiVeR, the IRON Sculptures hiDDeN in the weeds and all of theiR Buildings (weldiNg studio, vIDeo studio, painting studio, house, MILK BARN and ON and O

one of Julie's sculptures

LAWN

PeoPLe eatiNg snacks cocktaiL

6.26

Pigeons

are quite beautiful but also somehow repulsive maybe it's their obsession with food or their naked, parboiled feet, the homeless of the animal world.

Top Ten Reasons to Become a Bike Messenger:

1. Get in really good shape + get paid for it.
2. Wear really cool + bizarre clothes like a superhero.
3. Learn how to lock a bike really fast.
4. Read other people's mail.
5. Meet many cute receptionists.
6. Get to curse + spit at work.
7. Walkie-talkies.
8. Get to hit cab drivers with a pump.
9. Maybe be in 2004 Olympics
10. That's enough.

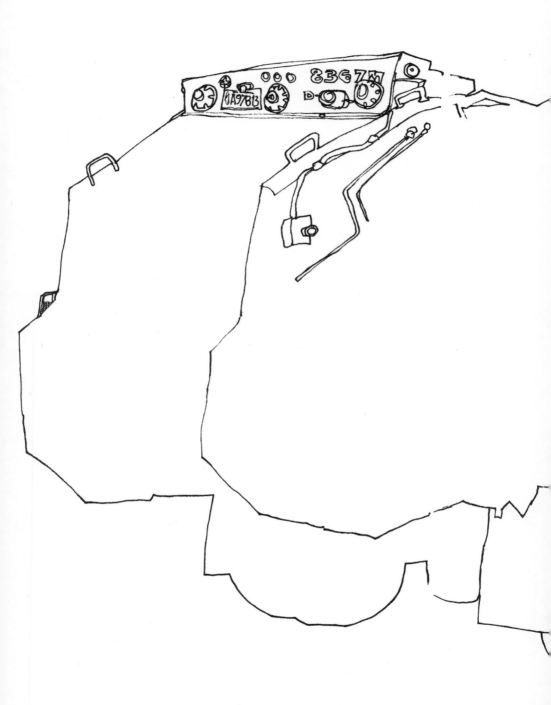

WRITING THIS BORING CRAP
and DRAWING ineptly have become fun
and something I feel an actual NEED to
do. So if I haven't written page after
page of crackling witty insight and my
drawings look like they were done by a
monkey using a stick up his anus, SUE
ME. Maybe one day, I'll do better. Maybe
NOT. In the meantime, I Like this, It
makes me better to myself, makes me
RECONSIDER a lot of things in my Life,
makes me take some risks and open some
DOORS. This new path is too short for
the view to be different from where I
was except in my fantasies, so rather
than dash them, I shall continue DOWN it,
and the landscape will change.

"SICK"®

That's what I told 'em at the office this sunny Thursday morning.
Sick of advertising
· Ford Motor Co.
· my office
· client comments.

I need a healthy dose of P+D: Patti & drawing.

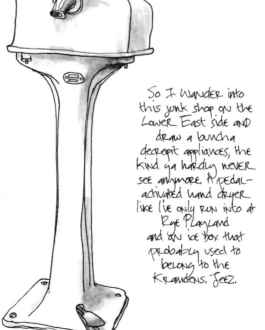

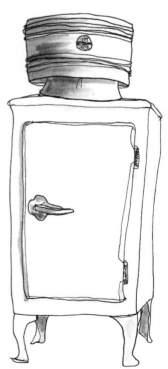

So I wander into this junk shop on the Lower East Side and draw a buncha decrepit appliances, the kind ya hardly never see anymore. A pedal-activated hand dryer like I've only run into at Rye Playland and an ice box that probably used to belong to the Kramdens. Jeez.

Mum's woods are alive and a constant reminder of the sterility of my regular environment. There are so many shades of green in the trees and plants, the sun is always changing the shadows and highlights, and a constantly shifting cast of beetles, ants, and spiders are hell-bent on reminding me that I am bugging them. I kill as many of the creepy bastards as I can.

I AM a NEW YORKER.

Lying on the floor and drawing over my head was the most painful way I could think of but I wanted to try something completely different. To make it more uncomfortable still, I drew our dining-room light while they were on, staring into the burning red bulbs for as long as I could, Then I added a final humiliation: my 3.0 Sakura pen which has a chisel tip and always makes graceless, ugly lines.

Despite all these indignities and the lousy drawing that I made, I had fun. That's the point of it all, a point I have been prone to forget during the months it took me to fill this book in my occasional detours into would-be professionalism. All these attempts to create functional reasons for my drawings all ended up in frustration and, for a while at least, led me away from the real purpose of all this "work" which is very simple and something I have craved and searched for these many years: to be.

Golden light through my shades. Laughter coming from Jack's room. The prospect of a nice hot cuppa tea. So far, not a bad day.

View from the front of St. Mark's church in the Bowery

(which ain't on the Bowery by the way)

A friend told me you don't have to draw only what you see so I added something special to this view

Like Andy W., I collect cookie jars. Well, one cookie jar. Unlike Andy W., my beautiful wife gave mine to me. And he's dead, I'm not! And he was a great artist and I have one cookie jar. But many cookies that I am still able to eat. And do. Hence my voluminous, crumb-covered gut. Unlike Andy W.'s.

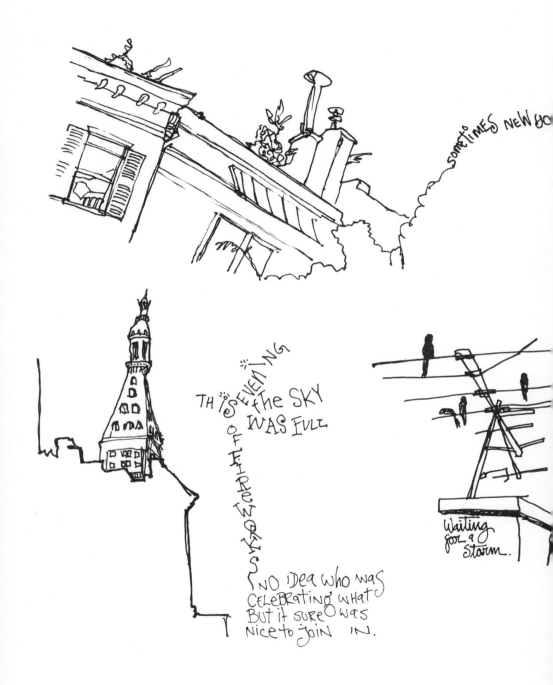

sometimes NEW YO

THIS EVENING the SKY WAS FULL OF FIREWORKS

Waiting for a Storm.

NO idea who was CELEBRATING WHAT BUT it sure was Nice to join IN.

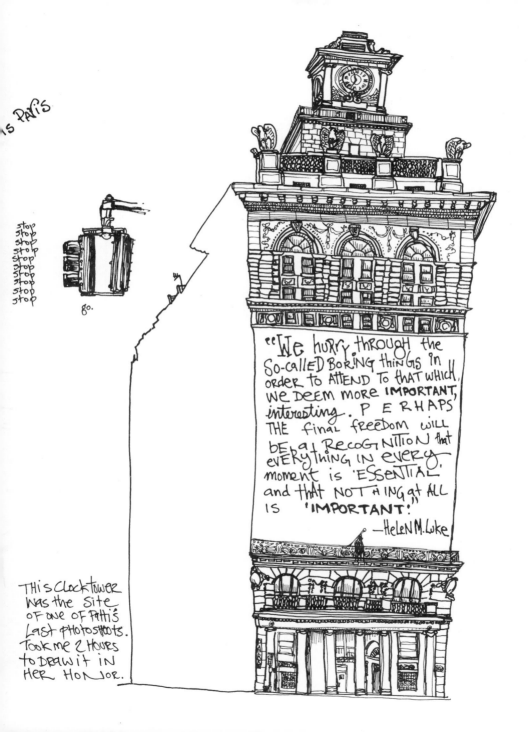

is PaRis

stop
stop
stop
stop
stop
stop
stop
stop

go.

"We hurry through the so-called boring things in order to attend to that which we deem more IMPORTANT, interesting. P E R H A P S THE final freedom will be a RecogNition that everything in every moment is 'ESSENTIAL' and that NOTHING at ALL IS 'IMPORTANT.'"

—Helen M. Luke

This Clock tower was the site of one of Patti's last photoshoots. Took me 2 Hours to draw it in her Honor.

THE FIRST THING I see
WHEN I CRAWL OUT OF THE
SUBWAY EACH MORNING.

Patti's Grandmother's
spice rack.

did you happen to see the

NOTH

THE TREES ON
MY BLOCK
FINALLY
HAVE ALL THEIR
GREENERY.

I JUST
sat DOWN
IN a BaD
MOOD + SaID,
"there's just

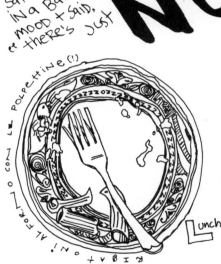

Lunch.

to

HE Lay
Limp
ON the
SIDEWALK,
IGNORING
ANYONE

...utiful GARBAGE TRUCK IN the WORLD?

PIZZA
PIZZA

"IF IT comes out Looking Like ART, it must Look Like Someone ELSE'S ART" - CHUCK CLOSE

N8

MILD headache

DRAW.

quail.

COOL PHONE @ EISENBERG'S Sandwich SHOPPE.

WHO TRIED to DISTRACT HiM from His misery.

ALRIGHT, a COUPLE THINGS. LAY OFF, WOULDYA?

BUSINESS TRAVEL

CAN BE A CRUSTY GAME. The TRIP'S NOTHING GLAMOROUS AND WHEN you arrive... you go to a meeting.

I like this drawing. Is that okay to say?

NO REAL SENSE OF HAVING **BEEN** ANYWHERE, JUST A LOT OF DISORIENTATION. LIKE BEING STUCK IN A REVOLVING DOOR with a PACK OF PEANUTS.

A BUSLOAD HEADING TO RIKERS ISLAND LOCKUP. I'M GOING TO JFK. GEE.

My PLANE SMELLED LIKE A SEPTIC TOILET. THIS IS ITS BOTTOM.

TAXI!

taxi to the AIRPORT.
taxi FROM the AIRPORT.
Taxi to the HOTEL.
taxi to the MEETING.
Taxi to the RESTAURANT.

A COWBOY CHECKS HIS GATE.

taxi to the HOTEL.
taxi to ANOTHER meeting.
taxi to the HOTEL.
taxi to the AIRPORT.
taxi FROM the AIRPORT.

RAMBLIN' BUSINESS MAN PARIS

I was BORN IN ENGLAND, GREW UP IN AUSTRALIA, PAKISTAN, ISRAEL... I MOVED SO MUCH AS A KID* THAT I SOON LEARNED TO HATE TRAVEL. SO EVEN THOUGH I TRAVELED QUITE A LOT FOR MY JOB, I NEVER EXPLORED. I WENT TO Japan and ate at BURGER KING. I WENT TO MELBOURNE AND ate ROOM SERVICE.

BUT NOW THAT I'M D R A W I N G, I CAN'T WAIT TO See NEW PLACES. I EVEN ENJOY AIRPORTS!

Waiting at JFK. this guy was on the phone but this is all I ever saw of him.

MORE TO SEE, MORE WORLD.

In a few weeks, I'm going to Nevada to visit Death Valley. In the summer, it reaches 140° but at this time of year we're hoping for warmish days, cool nights, ghost towns, abandoned mines, cacti, lizards, and tons of cool stuff to draw.

I'm **sick to death** of scarves, quilts, cold toes, rain, snow, wind, ice, blah, blah. I'm a bit nervous about camping in the desert but I get nervous about most things. Maybe a week in a GODFORSAKEN place will bake the HESITATION out of me for GOOD.

Escape.

OR, at least, dream.

It's been raining like a bastard this winter. Patti rarely uses an umbrella.

M, RIGHT.

THIS is the opening set of David Mamet's new Play, "The Old Neighborhood." A little boring. Let's hope the play isn't.

WANDERING ON 5th ave. Struck By how odd these water towers lookeD, aimed Up at the cleaR Blue FebRuaRy sky.

e, I've drawn an automobile that's more or less "proportion."

DOG 1

THis old 1940-something FIRE ENGINE came FROM A SCRAPYARD IN SEWARD, ALASKA. A SCULPTOR NAMED GREG POWLESLAND traded 3 months WORK IN the yard FOR the CAB and the CHASSIS + TURNED them into this mobile studio He could use in the wilderness. The CABIN is 7½ x 13½ feet. The EXTERIOR is designed to look like A HORSEBOX So NO ONE will buy HIM. GREG DID all the WOODWORK IN SPRUCE and Red CEDAR using only HAND TOOLS. IT HAS A CAST IRON, WOOD BURNING STOVE and MANY other COOL OLD THINGS He FOUND along the way. He has DRIVEN IT THROUGH AlASKA, the YUKON, BRITISH COLUMBIA then DOWN TO CALIFORNIA and across to BOSTON.

INDEED, SHE MAY. BUT THE TECOPA GRAVEYARD SHE LAY IN WAS FAR FROM DELIGHTFUL.

Loving Wife & Mom

VIRGINIA MAY DELIGHT

JULY 27
1918

JAN. 10
1992

MUD, CINDER BLOCKS, AND FADED PLASTIC BOUQUETS ADORNED THE DOZEN OR SO GRAVES.

FAITH COMMUNITY CHURCH

Dead Places

NEAR

Death Valley

TECOPA, CA.
JUST NORTH OF IBEX PASS, WHERE FOLKS WORSHIP UNDER A TIN-CLAD STEEPLE.

I WENT ON A 10 DAY DRAWING TRIP WITH MY GOOD BUDDY D. PRICE. DID MY FIRST WATERCOLORS IN THE DESERT.

ALL WASHED UP.

LAUNDRY

U + WE WASH

THIS COOL OLD LAUNDROMAT WAS UP ON A ROADSIDE HILLTOP. CLOSED FOREVER, ALAS.

THE BURRO INN CASINO AND RV PARK ACROSS THE ROAD HAS "LIVE MUSIC" AND "THE BEST FOOD IN TOWN". BUT THE DESERT INN IS DESERTED, PAINT PEELING + SUN FADED. A LONE BRASS DESK LAMP STILL BURNS IN THE FRONT WINDOW. NO ONE'S HOME.

'BAMBI', A TINY AIRSTREAM TRAILER THAT SEEMED TO BE SOMEONE'S PERMANENT HOME AND, DESPITE ITS SIZE, CONTAINED ALL THE AMENITIES INCLUDING COLOR TV AND FULL SIZED WASHER + DRYER.

The CROSS IS → OBSCURED BY A GIANT THERMOMETER.

BEATTY, N.V. A GODLESS TOWN WITH A BROTHEL, A BUNCH OF LOW-RENT CASINOS, AND THIS EPISCOPAL CHURCH, WHICH I DREW BY THE LIGHT OF OUR JEEP CHEROKEE'S HIGH BEAMS.

639 CHICAGO/OH

the idea of WHEELCHAIR TRAVEL

seemed totally daunting, and I've looked
for all sorts of websites and books
(my favorite being "Wheelchair
Vagabond") on the subject. Then we
tried it and found we get to be the
first people to board the plane (and
last to get off), and usually get bulkhead
seats and royal treatment. Every place
in the world has different interpretations
of accessibility. Some are over-the-top
and virtual hospital rooms, others are
over-sized and luxurious. Sometimes we
are received with helping hands, other
times with shrugs. We've always
managed with any accommodations and
chalked it up to "adventure." Which is the
whole point of travel,
n'est-ce pas?

FRESH HAIRCUT

Jack has BEEN VERY excited about our "CaVaTioN" since He woke up this morning. We left our packing till the last minute But we made it and now we're on flight 612 headed for Halifax. Jack & PI are napping in preparation for the journey ahead.

Jack Likes to give BATMAN RiDES on this HUMMING BIRD FEEDER; nonetheless, it attracted one H. BiRD to feed. It was about the size of a BIG BEE.

NOVA SCOTI

There's some kind of white SCUM FLOATING on the surface of the lake this morning. A GERMAN with a GOATEE said it was from the water lilies. It's FAiRLY ViLE, Like SOMEONE ELSE'S BATHWATER.

BOY, it sure ain't ugly out Here.

These Lilies bob and weave in the breeze.

Like spectators trying to get an unobstructed view of the lake.

Farmers hanging out at the oxen barn at the farm show we attended.

ON WEDNESDAY, I flew across the POND FOR a MEETING. had KANGAROO for DINNER at the BLUE Bird then slept like a CADAVER... THURSday MORNING I SPRUNG out of bed + hit the TOWN.

INTERMITTENT sprinkles sent me into a shop to buy an OMBRELLA before I set out for the day. It NEVER RAINED HARD enuff to take the BROLLY out of my bag.

M A R B L E · A R C H
is only a couple of blocks from my hotel, the Churchill Intercontinental.

CRITICAL MASS" by anthony gormley.

Hung from "hard aw"

most of the work was figurative. I liked a couple of things.

This guy was black + metal + one of a couple of dozens sculptures (60 actually) having around the Royal Academy of Arts. I stopped in to see the SUMMER EXHIBITION. Anybody who considers themselves worthy can submit up to 3 works + most of them are for sale from anywhere from £100-50,000. most were sold.

This is the FIRST HOUSE I ever LIVED IN on Elgin CRESCENT near PORTOBELLO Road. actually, I'm not positive if this is actually the place as I'm a bit sketchy on the house number. In any case, it's ancient HI STORY.

E r o s

dozens of youths

PICADILLY is like Times Sq. with LESS CHARM + MORE TRAFFIC.

JUST ONE DAY to VISIT all of

LONDON

H Y D E · P a R K
seems far more manicured + cultivated than CENTRAL PARK. It is full of ARAB fam eating ice cream. the SUN is SHINING + I'm drinking tea.

WELLINGTON ARCH.

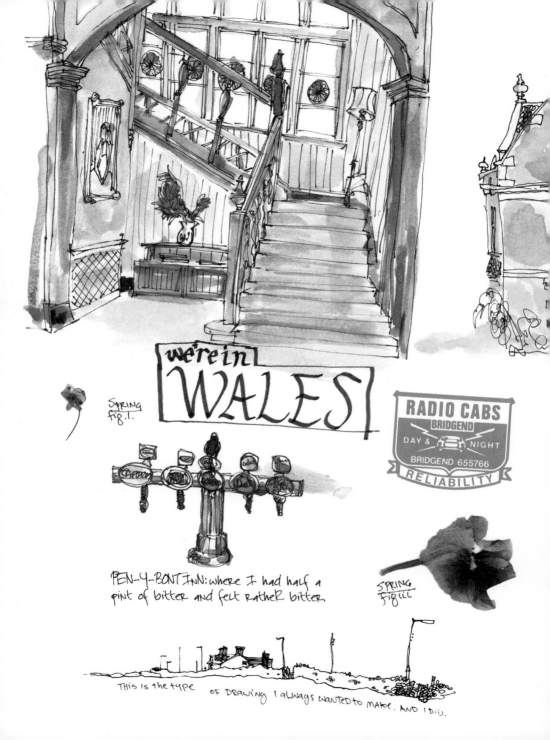

we're in
WALES

SPRING
fig.I.

RADIO CABS
BRIDGEND
DAY & NIGHT
BRIDGEND 655766
RELIABILITY

PEN-Y-BONT INN: where I had half a
pint of bitter and felt rather bitter.

SPRING
fig III.

THIS is the type OF DRAWING I always wanted to make. AND I DID.

cOed-y-MWSTWR: Our home here in the Vale of Glamorgan.

Welsh seems to have been invented by an awful
Scrabble Player with no vowel tiles.

It is very beautiful and sad; full of former coal
mines and miners now working in tech factories or
hanging around pubs. I've met quite
a few in the church and on the
farms I've been drawing.

There's nobility in their

past but I don't know

what their future will be

like but that's probably

a very American way

to look at things.

The Coach House

I have quite forgotten what a lot of these buttons and levers do. I have been word processing for too long and typewriters are as exotic as dip pens.

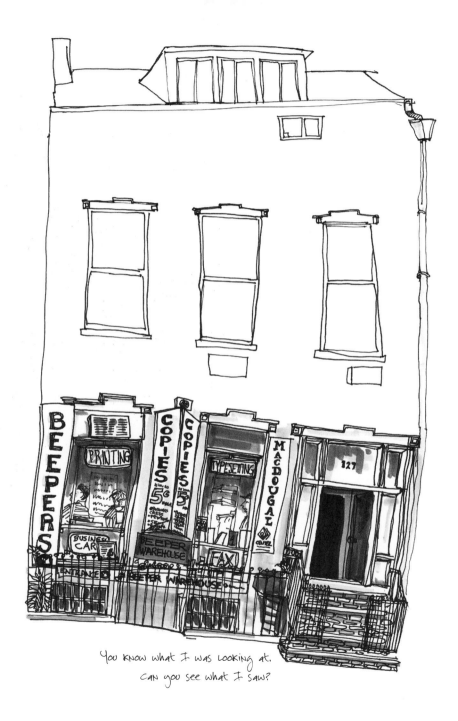

You know what I was looking at.
Can you see what I saw?

UNABLE TO RECONNECT WITH THE HIGHWAY, WE TOOK BACK ROADS MONTECATINI (SPA CAPITAL), PESCIA (FLOWER CAPITAL), SAN GENNARO (THROWING BASKETBALLS THROUGH TOILET SEATS CAPITAL) AND COLLODI (BIRTH PLACE OF PINOCCHIO'S AUTHOR'S MUM). THE TRIP TO **LUCCA** WAS WELL WORTH IT. A LOVELY TOWN (IN WHICH WE GOT HOPELESSLY LOST, OF COURSE) SURROUNDED BY A HUGE WALL, WHICH J AND I WALKED ALONG. I COULD HAVE SPENT A LONG TIME DRAWING ITS TWISTY STREETS AND CRUMBLING WALLS. WE MADE GOOD TIME ON THE AUTO STRADE BACK BUT GOT LED ASTRAY BY THE HIGHWAY TO ROMA AT FIRENZE AND GOT HOME AFTER SIX AND COOKED DINNER WHICH WE ATE AL FRESCO ON THE PATIO, BY CITRONELLA.

WE are in
ITALY
and, man,
it ain't Holland.

OUR TRUSTY GUIDE BOOK IS GETTING DOG EARED AND SWEAT STAINED.

1274 km.

DOESN'T SEEM LIKE THAT FAR UNTIL YOU CONSIDER HOW MUCH OF THAT DRIVING WAS AT 35 KPH DOWN TWISTING HAIRPIN CURVES ON STEEP MOUNTAINS WITH LUNATICS HEADING TWICE AS FAST TOWARD CERTAIN HEAD-ON DEATH. WHICH ISN'T TO SAY IT'S NOT FUN. GOING TO THE GAS STATION IS NOT FUN. IT COSTS ABOUT $4 A GALLON EVEN THOUGH OUR CAR USES DIESEL (WHICH I DISCOVERED SORTA BY ACCIDENT) AND ABOUT $50 OR MORE TO FILL THE TANK. YOU SLIDE CASH INTO A MACHINE (A REVERSE ATM) AND GAS UP.

PIAZZA DE SANTA CROCE and FRIES

FAST DRAWINGs of SNAiLs

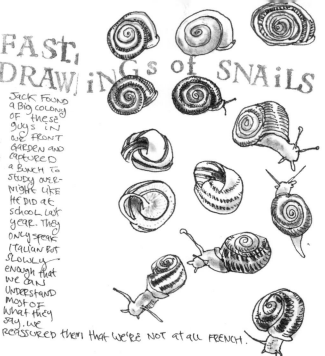

GIUSEPPE VERDI
Looks a little disappointed that we haven't been to any opera while in Italy.

JACK FOUND A BIG COLONY OF THESE GUYS IN the FRONT GARDEN AND CAPTURED A BUNCH TO STUDY OVERNIGHT LIKE HE DID at school last year. THEY ONLY SPEAK ITALIAN BUT SLOWLY enough that WE CAN UNDERSTAND MOST OF WHAT THEY SAY. WE REASSURED THEM THAT WE'RE NOT AT ALL FRENCH.

CHICKENS

YOU CAN DRAW THEM. YOU CAN FRY THEM.

I'VE RARELY SPENT AS MUCH TIME WITH AS MANY STUPID CREATURES!

They all have quite different faces but the same personality.

DO THEY KNOW THEY'RE ITALIAN?

— CIAO.

THE SUPERMARKET SELLS CHICKENS IN PLASTIC WITH COMPLETE HEADS WITH COMBS ATTACHED AND FEET TOO. THEY LOOK VERY ALIVE EXCEPT THEY HAVE BEEN FLAYED AND ARE WRAPPED IN PLASTIC.

EAT
EAT
EAT
EAT
SIT
SIT
EAT
EAT
EAT
EAT.

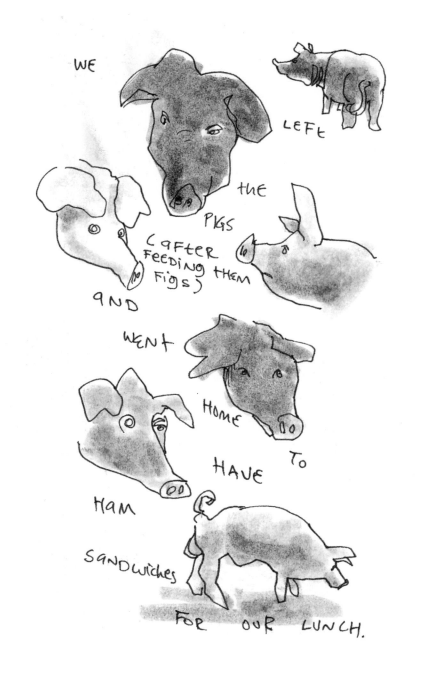

WE LEFT the PIGS (after feeding them FIGS) AND WENT HOME TO HAVE HAM SANDWICHES FOR OUR LUNCH.

ESSeNTIaLS

We go through at least a Bottle a Day. Sometimes, we drink From the Tap.

WE TRIED TO ARRANGE FOR A LAUNDRESS THEN I FOUND I HAD MARRIED ONE. I hang it ON THE LINE.

THE SUPERMARKET has an aisle FULL oF pasta. We STILL LOVE PENNE BeSE.

AS OUR LANDLADY SAYS, THE OLDEST WAY IS STILL THE BEST. NOT ONE BITE SINCE WE STARTED FIRING UP the COILS. IN THE MORNING, OUR ROOMS SMELL QUITE MEDIEVAL.

THREE OR FOUR ~ THREE TIMES ~ D

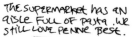

WE BOUGHt Big cups and DRINK it with milk + sugar.

a picture of
a pitcher of
peanuts

When Patti was in St. Vincent's,

I often found myself crossing the busy intersection of Seventh Avenue and Greenwich, a four-way higgledy-piggledy crossroad of death, and I just plain didn't look at the traffic or the lights. I felt like I had a get-out-of-jail-free pass, nothing more could happen to me now. I'd gone through enough. And if a close call made me realize that may not be true, it just didn't matter. Go ahead, splatter me. But the thought of my sweet Patti and the baby at home jerked me back into reality and more responsible behavior.

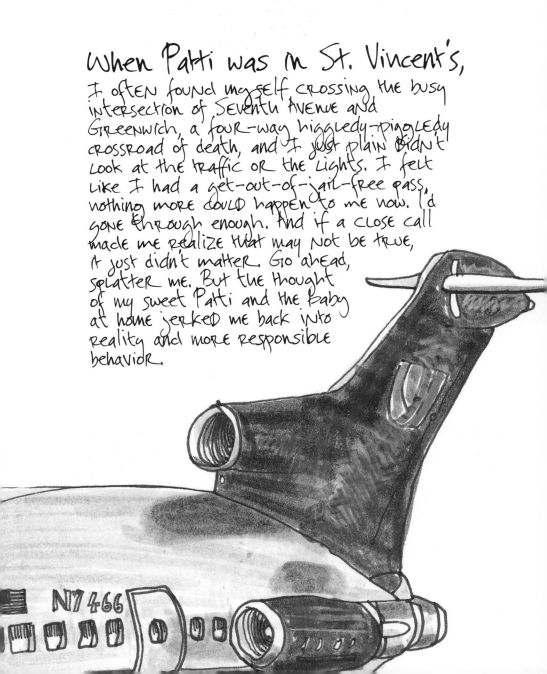

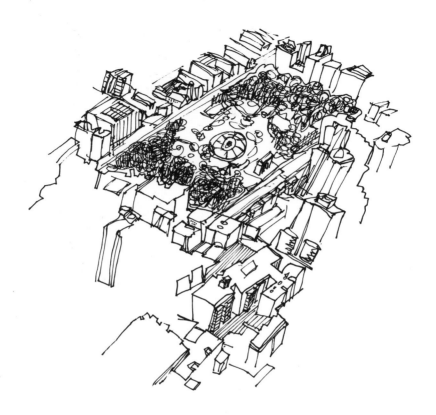

I haven't been immune to further tragedy, of course not. Many more horrible things have happened to my family and me, and they have been no less easy to deal with. Sorry, there wasn't some instant karmic revelation that let us all breeze through any hardship.

the most painful things for me are the fabrications of my mind. As Montaigne said, "My life has been full of terrible misfortunes, most of which never happened." What matters is not the prognostication and navel gazing, the theorizing and projecting, the what-ifs and the what-thens. What matters is today; all of the richness of my life seen as it really is and in 360 degrees. There is beauty in hospital waiting rooms, and I have seen it. There is beauty in funeral homes and cemeteries, and I have seen it too.

So many things happened to me that I never expected. And the bad things that I lived in dread of turned out quite differently than I thought. Life can only do to you what you let it.

Someone did a study of two groups, lottery millionaires and spinal cord injury victims. The research measured their degree of happiness, and immediately after the event, the lottery or the accident, there was enormous disparity between the groups. As you'd expect, the new millionaires were ecstatic, the cripples miserable.

But one year later, there was no statistically signif-icant difference between the two groups. There were miserable millionaires and happy gimps and happy millionaires and miserable gimps, all in equal measure.

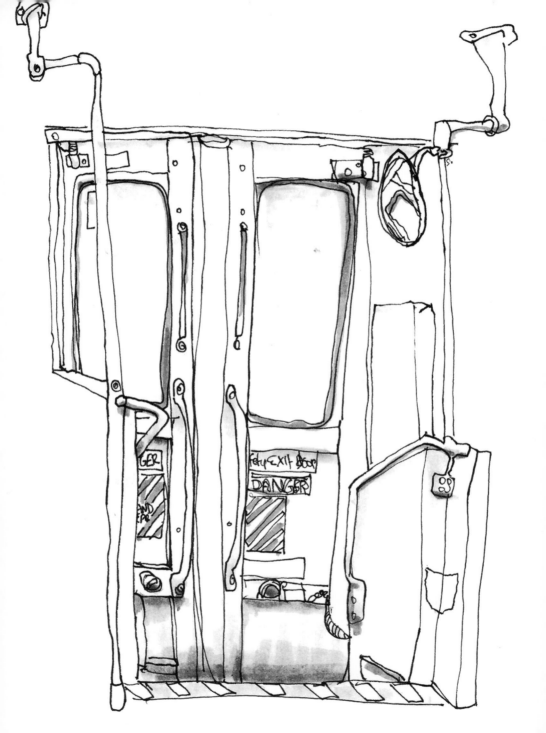

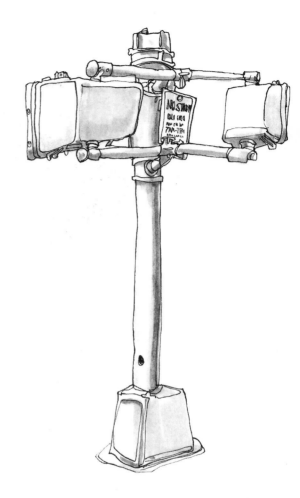

I don't draw every-day. Sometimes months will go by, and I haven't been able to stop and see and put it down on paper. I'm just too busy and distracted.

When I pick up my PEN again, my first DRAWINGS are horrible. cramped, tentative, blind.

But after a few days of steady practice, I am right back where I left off and I progress from there.

Each time I go back to really seeing, I SEE MORE.

I do love this hound.

Patti and I got him a few months after we met, and he was our first baby. He is always neat and trim with caramel paws and velveteen fur. He is intensely loyal, a staunch watchdog, and a great model whose only vices are pillaging the trash and hogging blankets. What a good dog, Francis Albert Hogman.

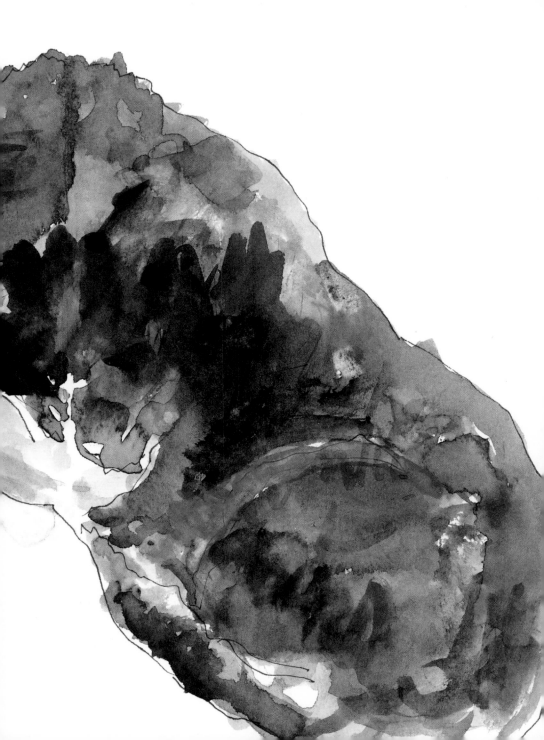

Pretty Patti

We can't control what life deals us, just how we respond to it. And if we are monomaniacally-focused on the bad stuff, we are missing the beauty of a half-eaten apple, the sunshine on the bedspread, the smell of warm cookies.

This is an important but slippery lesson, and I have had to learn it again and again. I still get the blues but, just like drawing, when I get back on the horse, I sit a little taller. Each time I get wiser, which isn't to say I won't be an idiot again next week.

Life changes, and you have to remain vigilant. The good thing is that when you fall off the wagon, it'll still be there waiting for you to clamber aboard again. I can always find a pen and a piece of paper.

Wise Patti

But most importantly and fortunately for me, I have an incredible woman at my side. She has had her ups and downs too, and our relationship has flexed and bowed over time but it never warps permanently.

or rips asunder.

We have been pretty patient with each other and genuinely wish each other well. What happened on those subway tracks happened to both of us and to many other people who know us, our family, our friends, and our neighbors. That shared experience has made it easier.

The fact that Patti is a magnet for people who love her smile and her giving heart has made it easier too as more and more people have joined our circle over the years. No burden needs to be shared alone if you can shake off your vanity and self-image and accept the help of people who want to give it.

Sexy Patti

Glamorous Patti

Baby Patti

At first, when I drew in the street, I was embarrassed and uncomfortable when strangers wanted to see what I was doing.

WOUNDED middle-Aged Gregory

RUBBER LIPPED "NOSTRIL" Gregory

But soon I found myself falling into conversations and friendships with many people who wanted to see what I saw.

Who, me? Gregory

I HARDLY KNOW Ma SELF.

I heard great stories and unusual perceptions.

and always found that they WERE Not what I thought they'd be.

PARANOID PORGY GREGORY

These strangers have given me the gift of themselves.

PURSED PABLO GREGORY

IN RETURN, I've given them, at least, my drawing.

HAPPY HEDGEHOG GREGORY

This story would not have been possible without loads of help from

a huge number of extraordinary people: daprice, Dr. Adam Stein at Mount Sinai; Fernando, Dot and Marie Barnwell at St. Vincent's, Bigelow chemists; Deb, Mike & Morgan Green, Hazel Kahan, Miranda Steiger-Murphy, Brian Murphy, Gran, Phyllis, Mickey + Bob Walahan, the Gladyzs, Dick and Dianne Dufner; the baby-sitting club (Sandra Robinson, Donna Bychak-Purdy, Ernie Lee, David Stevens, Steve Miller, Elliot Sokolov, and Graham Bellman), Dorit and Gilad, Anthea Simms, Dawn Kellman, Cindy Rose and Alan Kadet, Deedee and Chris Atkinson, Lynn Healy, Jennifer Quick, Bobbie Lloyd, Todd Rigby & VSF, Cynthia Tsai, Susan, Bob, Lulu and Dorothy Doran-Dye, Todd Oldham, Tony Longoria, Julie Salamon, Jennifer Thompson, Deb Wood, Jan Haux, Paul Sahre, Stefan Sagmeister, the Globus brothers, Helayne Spivak, Hollie McGowan, Mark Pinney & Laura Kane, John Hockenberry, Yvette Cortez, Ann Jorge, Phillipe Bertrand, Trish McEvoy, Marcie Bloom, Dean Holdiman, Mitchell Broder, Claire Treanor, Jack Orton, Maria Chandoah-Valentino, Dave at Madison Square Garden, Amy Fusselman and Frank Snider, Brent Weingart, Peter Laarman, Gianga Stone and our friends at God's Love We Deliver, our neighbors at 666 and 552, Shelly Donow, Joe Paladino, Efran Gonzales, David Jenkins, Bill Hamilton, Albert + Elizabeth Watson, Shelly Lazarus, Mylene Pollock, Texas East + Dot Giannone, Ben Watt + Tracy Thorn, Cheap Trick, R. Crumb, Hannah Hinchman, Betty Edwards, Frederick Frank, Ronald Searle, and all the strangers who generously and unconditionally offer help to Patti and other Disabled people on the streets of New York.

And, of course, Houndy (who we miss every day).